Literacy Strategies & Instruction
Grades K-12

Personalized Lesson Plans, Volume 1

Patti Gill

PORTLAND · OREGON

INKWATERPRESS.COM

Contents

Introduction

"Tell me; and I will forget. Show me; and I will remember. Involve me; and I will understand forever."

~Confucius~

Being in education for twenty years, and having had the opportunity to work with educators from kindergarten to twelfth grade, there is one aspect that remains consistent at all levels, the impact quality instruction has on student performance and achievement. The purpose of this book is to show you how to design, implement and facilitate teaching and learning. Once you understand the organizational framework to lesson design and instruction, you will then be able to easily adapt and incorporate any strategy successfully into your classroom.

Since NCLB, many teachers and schools feel the pressure to prepare for the state test; and in doing so, in some cases, that may mean teaching to the test. Quality instruction is the best test preparation there is. The detailed lessons in this book are aligned with state and national standards. Not only do they create authentic learning opportunities for students, but they also prepare them for the mandated testing required. Each lesson is written in a comprehensive manner using the before, during and after model that incorporates literacy strategies to enhance student engagement, while promoting reading, writing, speaking and listening across all content areas. The lessons are extremely versatile, and will allow you to modify and adjust them to meet your curricular needs. When done correctly, quality instruction allows the teacher to work with all students and minimizes the need for students to attend pull out support programs. My work is centered on the research and findings of Dr. Morton Botel's Plainer Truths and PCRP II framework, which have both been a part of the educational community for 25 years. He, along with his daughter, Dr. Bonnie-Botel Sheppard, founded and direct the Penn Literacy Network at the University of Pennsylvania. The Penn Literacy Network has greatly influenced my instructional practices and has taught me how to truly be a "facilitator" of learning. Their work has been impacting students, teachers, schools and districts across the country and globe for decades.

As you work with this book and use it with your students, I strongly encourage you to stop and reflect on your teaching, keeping in mind what I refer to as the *5 C's:*

Clarity= is there a clear focus on educational goals, desires and outcomes?
Community= is there respect for all people involved? Does everyone feel safe to contribute?
Communication= is there effective communication on all levels (teacher to student/student to student)?
Culture= is there a positive climate established where high levels of learning are expected, achieved and celebrated?
Commitment= is everyone dedicated and involved?

I love to ask teachers the following questions: *Would you want to be a student in one of your classes? Would you want to be a parent of a student in your class?* I ask these questions as a way to encourage reflection. We live in such a fast paced society and teachers are concentrated on meeting all the educational expectations, that sometimes "reflection time" gets unintentionally lost. When people, especially educators, stop and think about what they do and how they teach, that is when change begins and processes are refined.

I use the following questions to guide me through the planning process. I use them when I am planning for myself, or when I am collaborating with others. They are extremely helpful and focus instruction.

1. What do you want the students to know and be able to do?
2. What sequence of learning events need to take place to get them there?
3. What materials will I use or have available?
4. What strategies will I incorporate?
5. What kind of technology would enhance this learning?
6. How will they show me what they know?

After the lesson:

7. How did it go? What do I need to do for next time?

As you read each lesson, take notice of what the students were doing to reach the desired goal/objective. What would you do differently? What would your students need?

Remember, teaching and learning should be fun…for everyone!

Dedication

This book is dedicated to...

Brian, my husband and best friend---thank you for always believing in me and being my #1 fan! Your support, guidance and unconditional love made this all possible.

Kali and Corey---my two amazing children! Thank you for being so patient with me during this entire process. You are my inspiration and the reason I do what I do.

Kara---thanks for all your time, energy and assistance organizing this entire book. I don't know how I would have done it without you!

To all my family & friends----I am so lucky to have such an incredible group of people in my life! All your positive words of encouragement motivated me every step of the way.

To teachers everywhere----thank you for all you do for our children! Keep doing your best to ensure all students meet with success.

CHAPTER ONE
ELEMENTARY LANGUAGE ARTS: WRITING

The focus of this chapter is to take students through the writing process using a piece of children's literature as motivation and a model. The plans in this section will help your students become better writers, while preparing them for the state assessments. Research has shown that elementary students should participate in writing workshop a minimum of two to three times per week, for approximately thirty minutes or more per session.

Elementary Language Arts: Informational Writing
(1-5 Days)

:: Goals/Objectives

- Students will write a 4-paragraph essay about their favorite food, place or thing.
- This lesson can be adapted for younger grades as well. Look for modifications within this plan for assistance.

: Skills, Strategies, and Standards

Reading Skills

Main idea
Supporting Details
Summarizing
Synthesis
Connections

Writing Skills

Author's style
Voice
Paragraphs
Word Choice
Sentence Structure

Pennsylvania Standards

11.A.2.4.1
- Identify and/or explain stated or implied main ideas and relevant supporting details from the text

11.A.2.3
- Make inferences, draw conclusions, and make generalizations based on text

1.4.3 & 1.4.5
*Types of Writing

1.5.3 & 1.5.5
*Quality of Writing

1.6
*Listening to a selection of literature

: Materials

- *Pancakes, Pancakes* By: Eric Carle (children's literature book)
- Paper
- Pencils
- Journal/Writing folders if you use them

:: Lesson Plan

Before

- *Do Now*: Ask these questions to the class: *1)What is your favorite thing to do? Why? 2) Where is your favorite place to go? Why? 3) What is your favorite thing to eat? Why?* With younger children you can do this orally, but with older or more capable students I would have them pick one or all of the questions to respond to in writing.
- Discuss and share as a class
- Introduce the book, *Pancakes, Pancakes* By: Eric Carle. Tell them to listen carefully for the process and sequence Jack goes through to make his favorite breakfast, trying to remember as many details as they can.
- Read the book orally to the class and discuss (*What did Jack want to do? Do you think this was one of his favorite things to eat? Why? What did Jack do to get his pancake?*).
- Talk about informational writing

During

- Introduce expectations for the informational writing piece. Distribute template/organizer to each student (see below).
- Do any kind of brainstorming or pre-writing activities as needed to prepare the students for writing.
- Students will begin to write the introduction *(a model is included to use if needed)*.
- Students will continue to work on rough drafts.
- Revise and edit as needed.

After

- Students can type up or write final copies of their essays.
- Assess student performance using the criteria of your choice (state rubric, district/teacher expectations, etc.).

: Resources

* The book, *Pancakes, Pancakes* By: Eric Carle

: Possible Extension Activities

1. Compile into a class book---class recipe book, "Our Favorite Things", etc.
2. Have a class celebration where the students bring in their favorite thing, bring in artifacts from their favorite place, or make and share their favorite food with the class.

: References

N/A

Template for Early/Young Writers

Name _____

My favorite thing to _____
                (Eat)   (Do)   (Go to)

Is _____

To _____ this you need to
   (Make)   (Do)   (Visit)

_____

_____

_____

_____

I really like to _____ this when _____
     (Eat)   (Do)   (Visit)

_____

_____

_____

Writing Plan for Developing Authors

1st Paragraph (Introduction): Tell us about your favorite food to eat, activity, or place to visit, and include why.

2nd Paragraph (Body): Tell us how we can make your favorite food, partake in your favorite activity, or visit your favorite place.

3rd Paragraph (Body): Include all the necessary details and steps. Make sure it is sequenced properly.

4th Paragraph (Conclusion): Close by telling us the ideal time, location, or circumstances regarding your food to eat, favorite activity, or place to visit.

SAMPLE MODEL

Mom's Homemade Macaroni & Cheese

Do you have a favorite food or meal that you love to eat? Well, I do and I have to tell you that it doesn't come in a blue box either. Do you have an idea as to what it might be? I'll give you some more hints. It is made with elbow noodles and cheese. A small amount of milk and butter are added to make it smooth and creamy. Do you know what it is now? You guessed it; it's macaroni and cheese. Not just any macaroni and cheese, but Mom's homemade macaroni and cheese. It's the best!

Homemade macaroni and cheese almost has the same ingredients as Kraft's, but is made differently because it goes into the oven for thirty minutes or so. To make this delicious treat, you need: 1 box of elbow macaroni, 1 stick (1 cup of butter), and 2 cups of cheese (whatever kind you like, I normally use shredded cheddar), milk, a dash of salt and pepper and some breadcrumbs to sprinkle on top.

The first thing you need to do is cook the noodles. I cut the cooking time by two minutes to make sure the pasta doesn't get too soft and mushy. Then you need a 9 X 13" dish sprayed with Pam. Mix the noodles and cheese together in a bowl, place gently into casserole dish. Next, cut the stick of butter into small pieces and spread them evenly throughout. Pour milk over the noodle mixture until you see it peeking up through the macaroni. Sprinkle breadcrumbs on top and place in a heated 350-degree oven. It should bake for thirty minutes or until cheese is melted and the milk is totally absorbed.

My mom's homemade macaroni and cheese has always been a part of my birthday dinners for as long as I can remember. To this day, no family celebration is complete without it. It doesn't matter if it's Thanksgiving, Christmas or Easter, Mom's homemade macaroni and cheese is always the first dish to be eaten. My mom is not longer with us, but her memory and this family tradition lives on.

Elementary Language Arts: Narrative Writing
(1-5 Days)

:: Goals/Objectives

- Students will write a 4-paragraph autobiography about their life to date.
- This lesson can be modified for younger students. See adaptations in the lesson.

: Skills, Strategies, and Standards

Reading Skills
Main idea
Supporting Details
Summarizing
Synthesis
Connections

Writing Skills
Author's style
Voice
Paragraphs
Word Choice
Sentence Structure

Pennsylvania Standards
11.A.2.4.1
- Identify and/or explain stated or implied main ideas and relevant supporting details from the text

11.A.2.3
- Make inferences, draw conclusions, and make generalizations based on text

1.4.3 & 1.4.5
* Types of Writing

1.5.3 & 1.5.5
* Quality of Writing

1.6
* Listening to a selection of literature

: Materials

- *On the Day You Were Born* By: Debra Frasier
- Paper
- Pencils
- Journal/Writing folders if you use them
- Teacher sample of narrative writing following the template guidelines

:: Lesson Plan

Before
- *Do Now:* Have you ever heard stories about the day you were born? Do you remember what life was like when you were little? *(Do this orally with younger children and in writing with more capable students).*
- Share responses as a class.
- Introduce and read the book, *On the Day You Were Born* By: Debra Frasier orally to the class.
- Discuss book and introduce writing topic.

During
- Introduce and share expectations for narrative writing and distribute template/organizer to each student (see below).
- Do any kind of brainstorming and pre-writing activities to prepare the students for writing.
- Students will begin to write the introduction (you may want to write your own story to use as a model for the students) or share the student sample to use as a point of discussion. *What did the writer do well? What else would you like to know? What questions do you have? What would you do differently?*
- Students will continue to work on rough drafts.
- Revise and edit as needed.

After
- Students can type up or write final copies of their stories.
- Assess student performance using your criteria of choice (state rubric, district/teacher expectations, etc.).
- Share stories with the class.

: Resources
* The book, *On the Day You Were Born* By: Debra Frasier

: Possible Extension Activities
1. Have students write stories about their lives ten or twenty years later, from their adult perspective. This can be done in a letter to another classmate, in the form of a newspaper article highlighting major life events and accomplishments, etc.
2. Students can write poems about themselves and their futures.
3. Students can write 6 word memoirs about themselves.

: References
N/A

Template for Early/Young Writers

Name _____

    I was born on _____
                    (Month)   (Day)   (Year)

I live with _____

_____

_____

_____

My family is _____

_____

_____

_____

When I grow up, I want to be _____

_____

Because _____

_____

Writing Plan for Developing Writers

1ˢᵗ Paragraph (Introduction): Tell us your birthday, a little bit about yourself, and where and with whom you now live.

2ⁿᵈ Paragraph (Body): Describe where you live in detail. Giving many specific details so the reader can create a visual in his mind while he reads.

3ʳᵈ Paragraph (Body): Describe your life today. What is a typical day/week like for you? What are your hobbies? How do you like to spend your time?

4ᵗʰ Paragraph (Conclusion): What do you want to be when you grow up? Why? What do you hope the future holds for you? What are some of your long-term goals that you hope to accomplish?

My Extraordinary Life
By: Kali Gill

I was born on a sunny day in March of 1997. I am a very happy and funny person. I live with my mom, dad, brother and our pug, Mugsy. We live in Pennsylvania, in the suburbs. I love where we live because we experience the beauty of all four seasons and are close to beaches, lakes and cities.

My family and I live in a neighborhood with a lot of other kids and families just like ours. It can get quiet, but is a fun place because my brother and I have so many friends our age, and it is so easy for all of us to get along. The best time is when all the kids get together and play a huge game of kickball for hours. My house can get very busy in the afternoons right after school. That's because we have to get our homework done before we head out to practice. Most of the time, we only have an hour and a half to do it. At night, when the day is over, our house is peaceful and fun. We all sit together and watch T.V. snuggled under blankets with the lights dimly lit. I think it is a great place to live. I love my house!

A typical day in my summer life is I wake up to a breakfast cooked by my mom. Then I get ready to play with my friends all day. After my jam-packed day of never ending fun and games, I am ready to eat a big dinner. After dinner, I get a shower and then chill out. I usually go to bed around 10:30P.M. or 11:00P.M. One of my favorite things to do is making funny videos with my best friend, Steph. We hang out, play instruments, and sing too.

When I grow up, or even in the distant future, I would like to be an actress or sing with my best friend, Steph. I would pick that because I like people to see what I do and I like having attention. Both my goals, and what the future holds for me is my dream, which is to sing and act. I hope you got to know a little about me through this essay.

Elementary Language Arts: Persuasive Writing
(1-5 Days)

:: Goals/Objectives
- Students will write a 3 paragraph persuasive letter.

: Skills, Strategies, and Standards

Reading Skills
Main idea
Supporting Details
Summarizing
Synthesis
Connections

Writing Skills
Author's style
Voice
Paragraphs
Word Choice
Sentence Structure

Pennsylvania Standards
11.A.2.4.1
- Identify and/or explain stated or implied main ideas and relevant supporting details from the text

11.A.2.3
- Make inferences, draw conclusions, and make generalizations based on text

1.4.3 & 1.4.5
* Types of Writing

1.5.3 & 1.5.5
* Quality of Writing

1.6
* Listening to a selection of literature

: Materials
- *Excuse Me* By: Lisa Kopelke (Children's literature book)
- Paper
- Pencils
- Journal/Writing folders if you use them

:: Lesson Plan

Before
- *Do Now:* In writing, have students respond to the following prompt---***Do you or someone you know have some bad habit that needs to be changed?***
- Share responses as a class.
- Introduce the book, *Excuse Me* By: Lisa Kopelke. Make predictions and set the purpose for listening/reading. (*Frog has a little problem. Listen to find out what it is and how it gets solved.*) Read the story orally to the class.
- Discuss word usage and identify interesting words.
- Brainstorm as a class some habits people need or may want to change. *For example: burping, chewing with your mouth open, leaving lights on, not picking up your clothes, etc.*
- Talk about persuasive writing.

During
- Introduce expectations for the persuasive letter (see below) and distribute template/organizer. You may want to write your own letter to use as an example. One is included if you want to use it as a model.
- Begin writing introduction and include thesis.
- Students will continue to work on rough draft.
- Revise and edit as needed.

After
- Have student's type up their letters. They can add clip art or any other visual in the border that would enhance the effectiveness of their writing as long as it relates to the content of their letter.
- Assess student performance using your criteria of choice (state rubric, district/teacher expectations, etc.).
- Share letters with class.

: Resources
  * The book, *Excuse Me* By: Lisa Kopelke

: Possible Extension Activities
1. Compile letters into a class book.
2. Mail letters to the person they were intended for.

: References
  N/A

Persuasive Letter Outline & Expectations

1ˢᵗ Paragraph (Introduction): Greetings to the person who you are writing, a habit you want him/her to change, and the reasons why (thesis statement).

2ⁿᵈ Paragraph (Body): Your reasons with specific details as to why the habit needs to change. Try to make as many connections as you can to the person's life. Remember you are trying to persuade him/her to do something new. Be convincing.

3ʳᵈ Paragraph (Conclusion): Restate introduction and include your closing point.

SAMPLE PERSUASIVE LETTER

April 17, 2009

Dear Kali,

Being your mom is one of the greatest joys in my life; watching you grow up and become active in sports is so much fun. I love spending my weekends on a soccer field, softball diamond or basketball court, as long as I am with you. Your school and athletic schedules are becoming more demanding and the one habit that I think would really benefit you is to start doing your homework right after school, instead of waiting and putting it off. This will help you manage your time better, relieve some stress, and give you a chance to relax when you get home from your long practices.

I know some days you come home from school with a lot of homework. By starting it right after school while eating your snack, you can focus on the assignments without feeling rushed because it is getting close to bedtime. If you encounter a problem or are having difficulty with something in particular, we'll find out early on in the evening and have plenty of time to solve the issue. Being a sixth grader who is a member of three different travel sports teams can be hectic. There are times when you have two or three games per week, plus practices. Having an organized routine and set time for homework will definitely alleviate the pressure of something hanging over your head. The most important reason for doing your homework right after school is when you get home from a long practice you get to relax. You can play on the computer, watch a television show, or even have time to talk with your friends on the phone.

Kali, I am so proud of you and all your hard work! I care about you so much that I want you to start doing your homework right after school so you can manage your time better, relieve some stress, and have plenty of time to yourself to unwind after a long day. I love you very much and I always want to see you happy and healthy!

All my love,

Mom

Halloween Word Making/Creative Writing Lesson

: Materials

- "Halloween" letters on orange cardstock/oak tag
- Paper
- Pencils/pens
- Flashlights

Skills, Strategies & Standards:

Word Making Skills:

- Word patterns
- Word families
- Parts of speech (nouns, verbs, adjectives, etc.)

Writing Skills:

- Vocabulary
- Makes sense
- Sense of story (Beginning, Middle & End)
- Plot development
- Paragraphs
- Descriptive writing (using adjectives)

Pennsylvania Standards:

1.4.3 & 1.4.5
* Types of Writing
1.5.3 & 1.5.5
* Quality of Writing

:: Lesson Plan

Before:
- Distribute envelopes/baggies to each student. Using all the letters, see if the students can unscramble them to make one big word (Halloween).
- Once most/all the students spelled *Halloween*, introduce the word making activity—*using the letters, how many different words can you make? Halloween can count as the first word for everyone. Some other examples include: low, hallow, eel, on, all, owl, etc.*

During:
- Working individually, with a partner or in small groups (however you prefer), have students make as many words as they can and write them down on a piece of paper after they have created it with the letters. You can give them 15 minutes (more or less) depending how engaged they are.
- Next, have them put all their words into categories. You can turn this into a grammar lesson if you want and have them put the words into groups of nouns, verbs, adjectives, etc. Otherwise, you can let them make their own categories and be creative. The only requirement is that **all words** need to belong to a group.
- Share with the class
- Students will then write Halloween stories using as many words from their lists as they can. This can be done independently or "***progressive style***" among groups.

Progressive Writing:

Everyone starts out writing for a designated amount of time (5–10 minutes or so), and then they pass their paper to the next student. They read what is written and add their part trying to implement as many words from their list as they can. The rotations proceed until the student gets his/her original paper back. The student then reads the entire story and adds the ending. Students can underline, bold, etc. the words from their lists.

After:
- Students can pair up with a partner/group and share their stories…using a flashlight. Since it is Halloween, it might be fun to shut the lights out and have a few flashlights available for the students to use.
- Students can keep these stories in their writing folder to use at a later time for editing and revision purposes if you so desire.

Resources:
The Plainer Truths By: Dr. Morton Botel

: Possible Extension Activities
- Students can keep these stories in a writing folder to use at a later time for editing and revision purposes if you so desire.
- Pick one story element/literary device/writing skill to further develop. Use original story as a springboard for more detailed lessons and possible mini-lessons.
- You can do the same activity with other holiday seasons like, Thanksgiving, Valentine's Day, etc.

Directions: Print this on orange cardstock or oak tag and cut between each letter and put in a snack size Ziploc baggie or envelope (enough for each child, pair or group).

HALLOWEEN

HALLOWEEN

HALLOWEEN

HALLOWEEN

HALLOWEEN

CHAPTER TWO

ELEMENTARY MATH

In this chapter children's literature is used as a springboard for instruction in each lesson. Children's literature lends itself naturally to math instruction, and provides common background knowledge for all students. Literacy strategies are embedded in every lesson to enhance the problem solving experience. These lessons can be used as an introduction, extension or in lieu of a lesson in your current curriculum. Reflection sheets are also included to encourage students to write about their learning, which is such an important part of the process. I encourage you and your students to use math journals in class.

Kindergarten Math: Working with Sums of 10

:: Goals/Objectives

- Students will add numbers 0-10 to find all combinations of sums to 10.

:: Skills, Strategies, and Standards

Math Skills

Adding
Algebra (finding the missing addend)
Counting

Problem Solving Skills

Make an organized list
Use logical reasoning
Act out or use objects
Brainstorm
Use or look for a pattern

NCTM Standards

Numbers & operations
Problem Solving
Communication
Connections
Representations
Algebra

Pennsylvania Math Standards

2.1 Numbers, Number Systems and Number Relationships
2.2 Computations and Estimation
2.5 Mathematical Problem Solving and Communication

: Materials

The Very Hungry Caterpillar By: Eric Carle
Math paper
Counting bears or other objects (blocks) if needed to help visualize the process
Pencils

:: Lesson Plan

Before
- Talk about the number 10 and ask the class, *can you think of things that come in tens or have ten things?*
- Introduce the book, *The Very Hungry Caterpillar* to the class and set purpose for reading (*listen carefully to everything the caterpillar eats today*).
- Discuss the story and talk about the 10 things he ate on Saturday. Write the list on chart paper or on the board. If possible you can have the students work individually, with a partner or in small groups to come up with the list as well.
- Discuss lists and see if the students see any patterns or relationships. Ask them if they can make up an addition sentence that equals 10. For example: 5 oranges + 5 oranges = 10 or 1 apple + 4 strawberries + 5 oranges = 10
- You can play "Guess My Number" –you say a number and the kids have to tell you what number is needed to make 10.

During
- Students will work individually to complete the math paper below. If needed, provide students with counting bears or some other manipulative in order to help assist them with the addition.
- Go over as a class and say each equation orally.

After
- Discuss the skills and strategies that were used today. This can be done orally or in writing in math journals if students are capable.
- Discuss what was learned today about math and science (life cycle of a caterpillar, etc).

: Resources
- *The Very Hungry Caterpillar* By: Eric Carle

: Possible Extension Activities
1. Using the same math paper, you can begin to introduce place value to the class (ones, tens and hundreds). For example: if 1 + 9 = 10, what do you think 10 + 90 =?
2. Have students make individual books of 10. These are things that have 10 in them or come in 10. They can draw, use images, take pictures, and/or locate information using computers if you have access to them. This can be tied to other content areas as well. For example, if you are studying communities, students can find things in their community that incorporates the number 10. This can be done during center/writing time.
3. Have students do some research independently and at home on why the number 10 is so important. They will share this information with the class. Create a rubric of some kind to let students and parents know what is expected. Require a visual/objects/artifacts and some written component. You can make this as simple or detailed as you want. You can call it a "Brown Bag Report", where students bring in a brown bag filled with objects/artifacts that they will share with the class "show & tell" style. On the outside of the bag they will have their name, some facts or information about the number 10 and why it is important.

: References

N/A

Sums to 10

Name _____

Directions: Find the missing number. What patterns do you see?

Addend	+	Addend	=	Sum
1	+	9	=	10
2	+		=	10
3	+		=	10
4	+		=	10
5	+		=	10
6	+	4	=	10
	+	3	=	10
	+	2	=	10
	+	1	=	10

Second Grade Math: Bar Graphs

:: Goals/Objectives

- To provide experiences with gathering data, entering data in a table, and drawing a bar graph.

:: Skills, Strategies, and Standards

Math Skills

Compare and order numbers
Operations
Data analysis

Problem Solving Skills

Use or look for a pattern
Make a picture or diagram
Use logical reasoning
Guess and check
Act out or use objects

NCTM Standards

Numbers & operations
Problem Solving
Communication
Connections
Representations

Pennsylvania Math Standards

2.1 Numbers, Number Systems and Number Relationships
2.4 Mathematical Reasoning & Connections
2.5 Mathematical Problem Solving and Communication
2.6 Statistics & Data Analysis

: Materials

Caps For Sale By: Esphyr Slobodkina
Graph paper/blank bar graph chart
Pencils
Markers/crayons
Survey Sheet (see below)

:: Lesson Plan

Before

- Introduce the story, *Caps For Sale* By: Esphyr Slobodkina to the class. Do a picture walk and discuss what they think will happen.
- Set purpose for reading: *Who is this story about? What happened?*
- Read story orally to the class and stop at natural points to discuss.
- *Revisit questions from purpose setting.*
- Create a class bar graph to help retell the story (with the monkeys and color of caps) and introduce graphing concepts—*How many hats were in the story? How many monkeys were involved? What colors were the hats?*

During

- Students will conduct a class survey (see sheet below for guidelines)
- Students will individually create a bar graph to show class results.
- Students will share graphs in small groups.

After

- Groups and individuals will share results with the class.
- Compare class graph (from the story) to the student's graphs. Ask clarifying questions, What do you notice? What labels were used on the graphs? Why?
- Written reflection: What did we do today? What did you learn? What questions do you still have? What else do you want to know?

: Resources

- *Caps For Sale* By: Esphyr Slobodkina
- Everyday math resources from Lesson 3.5 on Data Pockets
- Class survey sheets

: Extensions

 * Use the money chart to practice/review working with money. This can be done during center time or as a separate math lesson/activity.

Class Survey: What Color Cap Would You Wear?

Name _____

Find the data.

  1. How many students are in your class?

Ask each student the following question. Keep a tally of your results.

What color cap would you choose to wear?

Color of Cap	How Many Students Would Wear It?
RED	
GRAY	
BROWN	
BLUE	

Caps For Sale Money Chart

Directions: Each cap costs 50 cents. How many different ways can you make 50 cents using pennies, nickels, dimes and quarters?

Pennies (1 cent)	Nickels (5 cents)	Dimes (10 cents)	Quarters (25 cents)
1.			
2.			
3.			
4.			
5.			
6.			
7.			
8.			
9.			
10.			

Second Grade Math: Place Value Practice

:: Goals/Objectives

- Students will practice and review place value.

:: Skills, Strategies, and Standards

Math Skills

Adding
Problem Solving
Place Value
Counting

Problem Solving Skills

Use or look for a pattern
Make a picture or diagram
Use logical reasoning
Guess and check
Act out or use objects

NCTM Standards

Numbers & operations
Problem Solving
Communication
Connections
Representations

Pennsylvania Math Standards

2.1 Numbers, Number Systems and Number Relationships
2.2 Computations and Estimation
2.5 Mathematical Problem Solving and Communication

: Materials

Knots On A Counting Rope By: Bill Martin and John Archambault
Colored beads or Rigatoni noodles that the kids can color or paint
Yarn or string
Paper or math journals
Pencils

:: Lesson Plan

Before

* **Do Now**: Ask your students the following questions: *How many of you have grandparents that you see often? How do you spend your time with grandparents? Why are your grandparents special?* This can be done orally if time is limited, or done in writing. For students who do not have living grandparents, use the following questions to have them respond to in writing: *1) Who do you like to spend time with and why? 2) Who is a very special person in your life? Explain. 3) Who is the best storyteller you know? Explain.*
* Share responses with the class.
* Introduce the story *Knots On A Counting Rope* By: Bill Martin and John Archambault and discuss how grandparents like to tell stories to their grandchildren.
* Read story orally to the class.
* Discuss the story.
* Tell students that they are going to create "A Story of Value".

During

- Introduce "A Story of Value". Have a variety of colored beads available for students to use. They can be the small ones you get from a craft store or the larger wooden ones you might have in your math kit. Assign a value to each color. For example, blue = ones, green = tens, red = hundreds and so on. You can go as high as you want or feel that they can handle.
- Students will work independently creating their own rope/story using color-coded beads.
- Students will swap ropes and try to figure the value of their partner's rope/story.

After

- Have partners share solutions with the class.
- Discuss the skills and strategies that were used.
- Have students write a reflection in their journals. You can use the following prompts as guides: *What did we do? What skills and strategies did I use? How will this help me with other math problems/activities? If they had difficulty, what was confusing? What do I want to learn more about? I could use some more practice with…*
- Students can also draw a picture of their ropes in their journals as well to help them with their explanations. You might want them to write a number sentence (equation) below it to have them practice their addition and double check their math.
- If time, share responses as a class. Otherwise, read student journals to see where you need to go next with place value instruction.

: Resources

- *Knots On A Counting Rope* By: Bill Martin and John Archambault

: Possible Extension Activities

1. The ropes the students created can be displayed on a bulletin board or used as a center activity to allow students further practice with place value and addition. You can title it, "Can you guess the value of my rope"?
2. Using their ropes, students can write an original story that incorporates math.
3. Students can build other ropes with higher levels of place value---millions, billions, etc.

: References

N/A

Sample

Can You Guess The Value of My Necklace/Bracelet?

I made a bracelet with the 4 wooden beads. Read the clues below to see if you can figure out the "value" of my bracelet.

Blue bead = I am an odd number with a 3 in the ones column and a 2 in the tens. What number am I?

_____

Purple bead = I am an even number that is one less than 11. What number am I?

_____

Green bead = I have a 5 in the ones column and the sum of my two digits is 12. What number am I?

_____

Orange bead = my number is equivalent to 4 groups of ten. What number am I?

_____

Answer Key

23 + 10 + 75 + 40 = 148

Use math journal or paragraph reflection sheet to debrief the lesson in writing.

Third Grade Math: Working with Money

:: Goals/Objectives

- To provide students opportunities to practice adding and subtracting money.

:: Skills, Strategies, and Standards

Math Skills
Addition
Subtraction
Money
Problem Solving

Problem Solving Skills
Use a table
Make a picture
Use logical reasoning
Make it simpler
Use objects

NCTM Standards
Numbers & operations
Problem Solving
Communication
Connections
Representations

Pennsylvania Math Standards
2.1 Numbers, Number Systems and Number Relationships
2.4 Mathematical Reasoning & Connections
2.5 Mathematical Problem Solving and Communication
2.8 Algebra and Functions

: Materials

Alexander Who Used To Be Rich Last Sunday By: Judith Viorst
Play money/coins to use if necessary
Paper
Pencils
Story Fact Sheet
Retelling Sheet

:: Lesson Plan

Before

- Introduce the story, *Alexander Who Used To Be Rich Last Sunday* to the class. Do a picture walk and discuss what they think will happen.
- Set purpose for reading: *Who is this story about? What happened?*
- Read story orally to the class and stop at natural points to discuss.
- *Revisit questions from purpose setting.*
- Explain and review the difference between a retelling and a summary. *A summary they want the main idea, and in a retelling they want specific details.*
- Hand out Story Fact Sheet and Retelling Sheet to each student.

During

- Revisit what a retelling is and explain how the Story Fact Sheet will help them.
- Do an example as a model to show them what they are expected to do.
- Students will complete their mathematical retellings individually or with a partner, whatever you feel is best.
- *The retelling is like a cartoon strip of sorts. Each block must contain a visual (an illustration), some words and a mathematical equation.* **For example**, *On Sunday Alexander received $1.00 from his grandparents. He bought gum for 15 cents. Now he has 85 cents left. $1.00 – .15 = .85*

After

- Share retellings with the class. This can be done in small groups or with a partner.
- Have students swap retellings with a partner. They will check each other's subtraction problems using addition.
- Complete math journal or paragraph reflection.

: Resources

- *Alexander Who Used To Be Rich Last Sunday* By: Judith Viorst

Alexander Who Used To Be Rich Last Sunday

Story Fact Sheet

His grandparents gave him $1.00 on Sunday

Activity	Money Owed
Bought gum	15 cents
Held his breath	15 cents
Rented a snake	12 cents
Said mean words	10 cents
Lost money in cracks	8 cents
Ate a chocolate bar	11 cents
Magic trick	4 cents
Kicked his brother	5 cents
Garage sale	20 cents

Alexander Who Used To Be Rich Last Sunday

A Mathematical Retelling

1.	2.
3.	4.
5.	6.

Third Grade Math: (Geometry) Figures & Polygons

:: Goals/Objectives

- Students will identify geometric figures and polygons.

:: Skills, Strategies, and Standards

Math Skills

Problem Solving
Geometry
Patterns

Problem Solving Skills

Use or look for a pattern
Make a picture or diagram
Use logical reasoning
Act out or use objects
Brainstorming

NCTM Standards

Geometry
Problem Solving
Communication
Connections
Representations

Pennsylvania Math Standards

2.6 Statistics and Data Analysis
2.8 Algebra and Functions
2.9 Geometry
2.10 Trigonometry

: Materials

The Patchwork Quilt By: Valerie Flournoy
Art supplies
8-½ X 11" construction paper
Geometric figures and polygons (cut out for students to use)
Tangrams (if you don't have a large supply of geometric figures for students to use, they can always trace tangrams)
Crayons & markers
Pencils

:: Lesson Plan

Before

- **Do Now**: Show students an actual quilt if you have access to one or show a picture of one. Ask students to describe in writing (in journals or on paper) what they see. What is a quilt? Its purpose?
- Share responses as a class
- Introduce the story, *The Patchwork Quilt* By: Valerie Flournoy and set purpose for reading (listen to find out what role the quilt plays in this story and family).
- Read the story orally to the class.
- Discuss the story. You can use the same questions from the "Do Now" to guide your discussion.

During

- Introduce the "Class Quilt" activity. Each student will create his or her own individual quilt square about an exciting or interesting event from this year. The goal of this is to have them incorporate as many geometric figures and shapes into their drawings as possible. You might want to specify a certain number that must be included (this can challenge them or give them an expectation as to what is required). The idea is to have the shapes look like they naturally fit into the scene. It's kind of like the *Where's Waldo* of geometry.
- Student will work on individual quilt squares.

After

- On the backside of the quilt square paper, have students list and number all the geometric shapes that they used. For example, 5 circles, etc.
- Put all the squares together to create one big class quilt.
- Display the quilt

: Resources

- *The Patchwork Quilt* By: Valerie Flourney

: Possible Extension Activities

1. Students can write the story that goes along with their quilt squares. These stories can be compiled into a class book and put on display with the quilt as well.
2. You can do some graphing activities about the quilt. For example, how many circles were used? How many triangles? How many trapezoids? Etc. You can have students create a variety of graphs and double check their accuracy using the information provided on the back of each square (where each student identified the number of shapes used).
3. Students can write poems about the quilt as a whole, or one for their individual square.
4. Students can work on persuasive writing, using the point of view from the lowest number of shapes used.
5. Students can write geometry stories…"A Day in the Life of a Rectangle" (and various other figures and polygons.) This can be informational or narrative form; whatever you feel would work best or is needed.

: References

N/A

Fifth Grade Math: Area and Perimeter

:: Goals/Objectives

- Students will calculate the area and perimeter of objects in the classroom. They will understand the difference, and be able to explain it orally and in writing.

:: Skills, Strategies, and Standards

Math Skills

Adding
Multiplication
Area
Perimeter
Problem Solving

Problem Solving Skills

Use objects
Make it simpler
Use logical reasoning

NCTM Standards

Numbers & operations
Problem Solving
Communication
Connections
Representation

Pennsylvania Standards

M5.A.1 Numbers and operations
M5.A.2 Understand the meaning of operations, use operations and understand how they relate to each other
M5.B Measurement

: Materials

Rulers/yardsticks
Graph paper
Chart
Pencils

:: Lesson Plan

Before

* **Do Now:** How big is your desk? What would you do to figure this out? Explain (you can use pictures and diagrams to help support your thinking). Share responses as a class

* Introduce the words **area & perimeter** if you haven't mentioned them yet in response to the do now question. Ask the students what they think each word means, which you can do via T-Chart. Circle the words or phrases that best describe what each word means. For example, *area = inside,* **perimeter**=*distance.*

* Have students find the area and perimeter of their individual desks using rulers/yardsticks. Share with a partner, and then as a class.

* Ask students what the area and perimeter would be if they put four desks together. Let them decide on the shape/location. For example, they could be 4 in a row or put into a square. You may want to distribute graph paper for this if you have some. Share and have them discuss what they did (process) and what they noticed about the numbers.

During

* Have students work in groups of three to measure rectangular objects in the classroom. Objects can include, an eraser, blackboard, textbook, pencil box, door, the classroom, etc. They will fill in the chart to record their work (see below).

* Have two groups get together and share their charts with each other. Make sure they explain what they did and how they did it.

After

* As a class, visit www.mathplayground.com. Click on "manipulative" and go on "Finding Area and Perimeter of Rectangles". Participate in the program and do some problems together for additional practice via the smart board.

* Have students complete the *Ticket Out the Door* in writing (see below). This will serve as their reflection.

* Have them respond in writing to the following prompt, ***why would you or someone else need to know the area or perimeter of an object, place or room?***

* Homework: Have students find the area and perimeter of 5 objects at home. They can use the same chart they used in class today. Make additional copies.

: Resources

* www.mathplayground.com

: Possible Extension Activities

1. Write an informational article for a math magazine on how teachers should teach area and perimeter to their students.
2. Area and Perimeter Grocery Store Trip---have students find the area and perimeter of rectangular objects found in a grocery store, like: cereal, hot chocolate, tea, etc.
3. Word problems with area and perimeter—using this link via the smart board. http://www.evgschool.org/areaandperimeterwordproblems.htm

: References

1. http://www.evgschool.org/areaandperimeterwordproblems.htm
2. www.mathplayground.com

Area & Perimeter Chart

Name _____ Date _____

Object	Length	Width	Area	Perimeter
1.				
2.				
3.				
4.				
5.				

Work Space

Literacy Strategies & Instruction: Grades K-12

Math Reflection

Name _____ Date _____

What did we do today?

How did we do it?

What did I learn?

Math Paragraph Reflection

Paragraph Brainstorming: List all the skills and strategies used to solve the problem you are writing about today. Be sure to include them in your written reflection.

Math Skills Used	Problem Solving Strategies Used

Today in math we had to _____

To do this I had to _____

_____

_____

_____

_____

_____

_____

_____

_____

Math Journal Reflection Sheet

Today in math I had to _____

_____

_____

To do this _____

_____

_____

The strategies I used were _____

_____

_____

The solution was _____

_____

_____

I learned _____

_____

_____

_____

CHAPTER THREE

ELEMENTARY SCIENCE AND SOCIAL STUDIES

This chapter shows you how to incorporate literacy strategies into content area learning. The content areas are the perfect places for students to practice and apply their newly acquired reading and writing skills. The lessons show how you can engage the students and get them to transact with the text to make their own meaning. Numerous note-making ideas are shared that encourage students to summarize the information they learned. This typically is a hard skill for students to master, but the more practice they get and the more ways we can show them how to do this…the better!

Kindergarten Social Studies: Where Do I Live?
(1-2 Days)

:: Goals/Objectives

- Students will learn about the various buildings and places found in communities.

: Skills, Strategies, and Standards

Reading Skills

Main idea
Supporting Details
Summarizing
Synthesis
Connections

Writing Skills

Descriptive writing
Word Choice
Sentence Structure

Pennsylvania Standards

11. A.2
- Understand nonfiction appropriate to grade level

11.A.2.4.1
- Identify and/or explain stated or implied main ideas and relevant supporting details from the text

11.A.2.3
- Make inferences, draw conclusions, and make generalizations based on text

11.1.B.3
- Understand concepts and organization of nonfictional text

1.6
* Listening to a selection of literature

: Materials

8 x 14" construction paper
The book, *Where do I Live* By: Neil Chesanow
Crayons/markers

:: Lesson Plan

Before
- Have students draw a picture of where they live on one side of an 8-½ X 14" sheet of paper. Encourage them to add as many details as they can. If they are able, have them label their illustration and write a few sentences about it.
- Share with a partner or as a class.
- Introduce book, *Where Do I Live* By: Neil Chesanow

During
- Read book orally to the class stopping at natural points to discuss, pose/field questions and make comments/connections per your class needs.
- When finished the book, discuss as a class: What stood out? What was interesting? What did you like? What did you learn?

After
- Have students draw things that they would add to their original picture based on what they learned in the story. Students should go back and add at least two more images/details that are representative of where they live.
- Students should write a few sentences about what they added and why. You can have them include their address as well. They can continue to practice writing their address during center/writing workshop time. If time permits, students can color their illustrations.

: Resources
  * The book, *Where Do I Live* By: Neil Chesanow

: Possible Extension Activities
1. Put students into small groups and have them create a small portion of a community/town. This can be done mural style and the kids can create an original name for it (maybe even incorporating your name too). If this is too abstract for them, you can have them create a replica of your classroom community first to illustrate the same principles and ideas.
2. Using the formula "Present + Possible = Future" have the students in the same groups, create what their part of the town/community might look like in the future. Again, this can be done mural style and hung next to the one done above. Then you can have discussions, using the murals as a springboard, as how towns change/evolve and why.
3. Introduce and discuss community helper's study.
4. You can even introduce map skills at this time, starting with a classroom or simple community map, and then gradually progressing to more complex and detailed versions of the state, United States, world, etc.

: References
  N/A

Kindergarten Social Studies: Community Helpers
(1-2 Days)

:: Goals/Objectives
- Students will learn about community helpers and the role they play in our lives.

: Skills, Strategies, and Standards

Reading Skills
Main idea
Supporting Details
Summarizing
Synthesis
Connections

Writing Skills
Descriptive writing
Word Choice
Sentence Structure

Pennsylvania Standards
1.4
* Types of writing
1.5
* Quality of writing

: Materials
Note-making sheets (located below)
Images/pictures of community helpers from Google or other resources you might have
Journals or paper to write on
Pencils

:: Lesson Plan

Before

- Distribute pictures of community helpers (from Google images, magazines, posters or from any other resources you may have) fire fighters, police, grocery clerks, crossing guards, dentists, doctors, construction workers, etc.
- Students can sit with a partner (either at desks or on the carpet) looking at their picture. Ask the following questions orally or in writing (see template below).
- Share out with the class.

During

- Using the pictures (and any other resources, or materials you might have with community helpers), students will write a short informational paragraph about their community helper based on what they know, what they've learned and what they see.
- They can use the template below to help guide them through the writing process.

After

- Share informational paragraphs with the class.

: Resources

N/A

: Possible Extension Activities

1. Compile community helper writings into class books. For example, All About Fire Fighters will be one book, All About Police, etc.
2. Invite various community helpers to visit the classroom as guest speakers. You can contact the local Kiwanas club members, etc.
3. Plan field trips to visit the workplaces of the various community helpers in your town.

: References

N/A

Community Helpers

Name(s) _____

1. Who is this picture of? How do you know?

2. What does this person do?

3. How does this person help our community and us?

Community Helper Writing Template

Name _____

Being a _____

Is _____

_____

Because they _____

_____

_____

_____

I liked learning and writing about _____

_____

Second Grade: Introduction to Literature Circles

:: Goals/Objectives

- Students will learn how to transact with text in preparation for literature circles.

:: Skills, Strategies, and Standards

Reading Skills
Main idea
Supporting Details
Summarizing
Synthesis
Connections

Writing Skills
Paragraph Structure
Descriptive writing
Word Choice
Sentence Structure

Pennsylvania Standards
1.1 A - H
- Learning to Read Independently

1.3 A - F
- Reading, Analyzing, and Interpreting Literature

1.5 A - G
- Quality of Writing

1.7 A - C
- Characteristics of Function of the English Language

:: Materials

Articles about the Great Depression and how it affected the children.
Photographs showing families during the Great Depression
American Girl books

http://newdeal.feri.org/eleanor/er2a.htm
http://newdeal.feri.org/eleanor/alc0138.htm
http://history1900s.about.com/library/photos/blygd32.htm

:: Lesson Plan

Before
- **Do Now:** Describe a typical day/weekend in your life and family. Include as many details as you can to give us a clear idea what you do and how you spend your time. If possible, try to have them write 5 lines/sentences in their journals.
- **Share** responses as a group/class.
- Tell the students that we are going to take a look at kids your age and their life a long time ago during the Great Depression, just like Kit 's stories.
- Talk about what the word "**Depression/depressed**" means. Brainstorm a list of words that they think mean the same as depressed. Circle the best ones listed. Discuss as a group/class, what life might have been like and what things could be happening as a result. If the group is aware and capable, you might want to make some connections to our current economic situation. This can be done after the lesson as well.

During
Hand out copies of the article, "How the Great Depression Affected Children" to each student. Make predictions about the text and introduce the 4 square note-making strategy (See attached sheet).

- Have students read the article silently first. Then as a group, re-read the article and fill out the 4 square sheets together to model for the students how to complete it.
- Start with the key words and fill that in as you read as a group. You can also fill in the connections section while reading, or you can do it after you are done the article.
- Have the students complete the summary section on their own. Explain to them, that you want them to summarize what they just read in a few sentences. They can incorporate some key words if that helps them.
- Have them finish the illustration block last. Ask them, "if you had to draw a picture/ symbol/visual to help you remember what you read about today, what would it be"? This may be hard for them at first, but it is really helpful and higher level thinking. Try to steer them to one image not an entire scene.

After
Reflect as a group on how you transacted with text today. Ask them the following questions:
- What did we do today?
- How did this help us with our understanding and remembering (comprehension) what we read?
- If you had to talk about what you read with someone, would the 4 square sheets help you?

: Resources
N/A

: Possible Extension Activities

1. Students can use the 4 square approach with other supplemental materials to help build background on other American Girl books.
2. The students can use the 4 square note-making strategy with independent books to help prepare them for future literature circle roles.
3. The students can use the bookmarks as they read to help organize them for literature circle roles. You can have them complete a chapter or two individually using the bookmarks, then assign specific roles to them in class. This way, they each get practice and become comfortable with all roles, while also being able to provide support to other classmates during collaboration time. This will help to make the discussions richer in content.

: References

Links:

http://newdeal.feri.org/eleanor/er2a.htm
http://newdeal.feri.org/eleanor/alc0138.htm
http://history1900s.about.com/library/photos/blygd32.htm

The goal of this lesson is to scaffold instruction in order to have the students become comfortable with all the roles involved in a typical literature circle lesson.

4 Square Note-Making Sheet

Name _____

Key Words	Connections
Summary	**Illustration**

Bookmark

Make these on cardstock or oak tag back to back. The kids can fill out one bookmark per chapter, every couple of pages, etc. based on individual needs or teacher direction.

Key Words

Connections

Summary

Illustration

Third Grade Animal Adaptation Lesson

:: Goals/Objectives

- Students will identify main idea and supporting details while learning about animal adaptations.

:: Skills, Strategies, and Standards

Reading Skills

Main idea
Supporting Details
Summarizing
Synthesis
Connections

Writing Skills

Paragraph Structure
Descriptive writing
Word Choice
Sentence Structure

Pennsylvania Standards

1.1 A - H
- Learning to Read Independently

1.3 A - F
- Reading, Analyzing, and Interpreting Literature

1.5 A - G
- Quality of Writing

1.7 A - C
- Characteristics of Function of the English Language

:: Materials

Snug In The Snow article http://dnr.wi.gov/org/caer/ce/eek/nature/snugsnow.htm
Index Cards
Paper/journals for each student

Post-its

:: Lesson Plan

Before

* **Do Now:** What is your favorite season and why? Give three reasons with specific examples. *(Summer because I get to go to my favorite place ever...the beach)* Share responses with the class/group.

* Introduce the word **adaptation**. Ask students if they know what the word **adap**t means (use it in a sentence to give them a clue if needed).

* Talk about how we adjust/adapt our style of living based on weather, etc. Example: In summer we go to the beach, go swimming, eat water ice and other things to stay cool.

During

* Hand out the article to each student. Make predictions about the text based on the title, *Snug In The Snow.*

* Have students read the article independently. After they read each paragraph, have them write down two words that best summarize what they read in the paragraph. The words can actually be found in the article, or ones that help them remember what they read. They can underline, highlight or write them in a journal. You might want to do the first paragraph together to model.

* After students have completed the article and wrote down their words on paper, put them —Post·its into groups (3 or 4 per group). As a group, have them come up with the seven key words that best summarize/describe the text and write them down. Have groups share with the class.

* Distribute index cards to students, one per person. Individually on the lined side, have the students use all seven of their words to write about what they read in the article. Make sure they underline each key word. Students should share their descriptive writing with others in their group. If time allows, have a few students share with the class.

* On the other side of the index card, have them write a one-sentence summary about *Snug In The Snow* (if you had to describe what the whole article was about in one sentence, what would you say?).

* Essentially, they just generated a "backwards paragraph", with the details on one side and the main ideas on the other. At a later time, you can hand them back during writing workshop to turn into a cohesive paragraph about hibernation/animal adaptations.

After

* Discuss and list the ways various animals in the article prepare for winter. You can do the same thing with humans via a T-Chart or Venn diagram.

* You can have them pick two animals from the article to complete a hibernation/animal adaptation Venn diagram for an assessment.

* Students will answer one of the following prompts in writing as an assessment check.

1. *How do animals adapt to prepare for winter? Give at least three specific examples to support your thinking.*
2. *What do animals and humans have in common as they prepare for winter? Give at least three specific examples to support your thinking.*

: Resources

Snug In The Snow (link listed above)
Two word summary by Linda Hoyt from her *Revisit, Reflect, Retell* book (1999 pgs. 4 &5)

: Possible Extension Activities

1. Students can do animal adaptation reports on the animal of their choice.
2. Pair non-fiction/fiction texts together as you explore animal adaptations.
3. Explore various countries, regions, states or any other area of interest and find out what they do, how they live, what they eat, industries, and other information based on their geographic location, climate, temperature, etc.

: References

Links:

EEK website: http://dnr.wi.gov/org/caer/ce/eek/nature/snugsnow.htm
Books:
Revisit, Reflect, Retell By Linda Hoyt (1999)

Writing Prompt Assessment

Directions: Pick one of the following questions to answer. Remember to write in paragraph form, provide specific examples and make sure you answer the question completely.

1. How do animals adapt to prepare for winter? Give at least three specific examples to support your thinking.

2. What do animals and humans have in common as they prepare for winter? Give at least three specific examples to support your thinking.

Fifth Grade Fossil Lesson

:: Goals/Objectives

- Students will be able to explain how fossils were formed and what information they provide us about Earth's history.

:: Skills, Strategies, and Standards

Reading Skills

Main idea
Supporting Details
Summarizing
Synthesis
Connections

Writing Skills

Paragraph Structure
Descriptive writing
Word Choice
Sentence Structure

Pennsylvania Standards

1.1 A - H
- Learning to Read Independently

1.5 A - G
- Quality of Writing

1.7 A - C
- Characteristics of Function of the English Language

:: Materials

Paper
Crayons, markers, colored pencils
Computer links listed in lesson
Note-making sheets
Informational articles on fossils
Display table with "fossil vs. non-fossil" objects

:: Lesson Plan Day One

Before

Have students respond to the following prompt in writing.

- **Do Now:** Describe what the world looked like millions of years ago. What animals were living? What types of plants were around? Etc.
- Share responses. Ask students, "How do you know the world looked like that?" "What evidence has been shown?" Etc.
- Introduce the word **"paleontology"** and tell the students they are going to be thinking and working like a paleontologist today.

During

* Have students read and complete the "What is a fossil?" article and note-making sheet.

* Have students share responses/note-making sheets with a partner or in small groups.

* Students will write a paragraph using the sheet to help them.

* While the students are working on their paragraphs, have small groups come up to visit your display table. Set up a display table with some of the following objects dispersed randomly about. Also place two cards on the table, one that says "fossils" and one that says "non-fossils". Ask the students to observe the objects on the table and try to pick out the "fossils" from the "non-fossils" mentally. Give them a few minutes and then bring up the next group.

Display Table

Fossils = any real/replica fossil that you can get your hands on, or you can always Google images and mount them on paper.

Non-fossils = metamorphic rock, igneous rock, plastic bottle, bone, shell, stuffed dinosaur, paper towel, piece of wood, piece of metal, etc.

After

* Have a few students share their paragraphs orally with the class, with a partner or in small groups. Collect them to review and grade/assess.

: Resources

- See links below for resources used to design and create this lesson.
- See attachments for resources needed to complete this lessons.

: Possible Extension Activities

- Crossword Puzzles (www.fossilsfacts-and-finds.com)
- Life Story of a Fossil (from the paleontology portal) http://www.ucmp.berkeley.edu/education/lessons/fossilstory/fossilstory.html Click on handout and worksheet for details.
- Make an original fossil to go along with their story.
- Creative Writing Ideas
- http://www.acad.carleton.edu/curricular/BIOL/classes/bio302/Pages/CreativeWritingIdeas.html

: References

* See links above for references used to design and create this lesson.

Name _____ Date _____

What Is a Fossil?

Article From: http://www.windows.ucar.edu/tour/link=/earth/geology/fossilintro.html

Fossils are evidence of ancient life preserved in sedimentary rocks. On Earth, they are clues to what living things, ecosystems, and environments were like in the past. The oldest fossils are from mats of blue-green algae that lived over three billion years ago. The youngest fossils are from animals that lived before the beginning of recorded history, 10,000 years ago.

Scientists that study fossils know that the types of creatures that lived on the planet at different times in Earth history have changed quite a bit over millions and millions of years. Each unique type of life form, whether alive today or extinct, is called a species. Most fossils are from species that no longer live on the planet because they have become extinct. Many of these extinct species are somewhat similar to species that live today.

Fossils are not always big dinosaur bones or fancy shells like the ones found in museums. In fact, if you think you have never found a fossil, think again! You probably rely on fossils everyday by using fossil fuels such as oil, gas, or coal to power cars, lights, and heat or cool your house. Fossil fuels are organic carbon from ancient plants and marine life that lived millions of years ago. So, every time you pull into a gas station, think about the fossils that are filling the tank!

Body fossils are remains of actual organisms. Most living things never become fossils. It takes special conditions for a fossil to form. Hard parts made of mineral such as shells and bones are much more likely to become body fossils than soft tissues, such as skin, organs, and eyes, which usually decay. This means that animals like jellyfish, which have no bones made of hard mineral, are rarely preserved.

Trace fossils are clues to how ancient animals lived. For instance, if you were to make footprints on the beach today and the beach sand eventually became cemented together forming a rock called sandstone, your footprints would be in the rock as well. They would be trace fossils and evidence that you were once there. This doesn't happen very often. Think about all the people, dogs, crabs, birds and other animals that walk over a beach each day. Few, if any, of those footprints will become fossils someday. Most of them are washed away by wind and waves. Other examples of trace fossils include crab burrows, dinosaur bite marks, and bear claw starches on the walls of caves.

Fossil Note-Making Sheet

Name _____ **Date** _____

Topic: Fossils

List interesting facts and details about fossils as you read the article.

1.

2.

3.

4.

5.

6.

7.

Describe what a fossil is in one sentence below.

A fossil is _____

_____

ON A SEPARATE PIECE OF LINED PAPER, WRITE A PARAGRAPH ABOUT WHAT YOU LEARNED ABOUT FOSSILS. USE THE INFORMATION ON THIS SHEET TO HELP YOU.

Fifth Grade Fossil Lesson

:: Goals/Objectives

- Students will be able to explain how fossils were formed and what information they provide us about Earth's history.

:: Skills, Strategies, and Standards

Reading Skills

Main idea
Supporting Details
Summarizing
Synthesis
Connections

Writing Skills

Paragraph Structure
Descriptive writing
Word Choice
Sentence Structure

Pennsylvania Standards

1.1 A - H
- Learning to Read Independently

1.5 A - G
- Quality of Writing

1.7 A - C
- Characteristics of Function of the English Language

:: Materials

Paper
Crayons, markers, colored pencils
Computer links listed in lesson
Note-making sheets
Informational articles on fossils
Display table with "fossil vs. non-fossil" objects

:: Lesson Plan Day Two

Before

Have students respond to the following prompt in writing.

- **Do Now:** Have the display table where all students can see it or you can have students stand around it or sit at their seats. Have them make a T-Chart labeled "Fossils" and "Non-Fossils", then list the objects on the table in the proper columns.
- Share responses and discuss characteristics of each group as a class.
- Review what they learned about fossils yesterday orally.
- Explain that today they are going to learn how fossils are formed.

During

- Hand out article, "What is a fossil? How do they form?" (http://www.discoveringfossils. co.uk/whatisafossil.htm) and a blank sheet of 8 1/2 X 11" plain sheet of paper. Have them fold the paper so they have 6 squares on one side.
- Students will read the article (this can be done independently, in small groups, with a partner or as a class) and then create an original cartoon strip on how fossils are formed. Students can get creative as they want with this. Encourage them to use "proper paleontology vocabulary" as well.
- If time allows, have them color their illustrations to add more detail. They can also use the worksheet as a rough draft and complete a good copy on white construction paper.
- Share cartoon strips with a partner or in small groups.

After

As a class, complete "Getting Into Fossils Record" Level 1 Student (link listed below in resources) as a class via smart board. You can have them write the answers to the review on paper individually, with a partner or work in small groups and utilize it as a "game-like" review. You can give a traditional paper/pencil test or quiz the following day or two.

: Resources

- See attachments for resources needed to complete this lesson.
- http://www.ucmp.berkeley.edu/education/explorations/tours/fossil/

: Possible Extension Activities

- Crossword Puzzles (www.fossilsfacts-and-finds.com)
- Life Story of a Fossil (from the paleontology portal) http://www.ucmp.berkeley.edu/ education/lessons/fossilstory/fossilstory.html Click on handout and worksheet for details.
- Make an original fossil to go along with their story.
- Creative Writing Ideas
- http://www.acad.carleton.edu/curricular/BIOL/classes/bio302/Pages/ CreativeWritingIdeas.html

: References

* See links above for references used to design and create this lesson.

Fifth/Sixth Grade Study Skills: Science Lesson

:: Goals/Objectives

- Students will read and understand the organization of informational text to assist with test taking strategies.

:: Skills and Standards

Reading Skills

Main Idea
Inferencing
Essential/Non-essential information
Drawing Conclusions
Relevant Details

Writing Skills

Paragraph Structure
Descriptive writing
Word Choice
Sentence Structure

Pennsylvania Standards

R 11. A. 2.6 Identify, describe and analyze genre of text
R 11. A. 2.3 Make inferences, draw conclusions, and make generalizations based on text
R 11. A. 2.3.2 Cite evidence from text to support generalizations
R 11. B.3.3.1 Explain, interprets, and/or analyzes the effect of text organization, including the use of headers

:: Materials

Copy of the article for each student to use (see link below).
Teacher copy of the article
Highlighters
Journals/reflection sheet

Link:

http://discoverer.prod.sirs.com/discoweb/disco/do/article?urn=urn%3Asirs%3AUS%3BARTICL E%3BART%3B0000176060

:: Lesson Plan

Before

Have students respond to the following in writing.

- Write the words *"swimming"* and *"Antarctica"* on the board (next to each other or T-Chart style).
- As a class or individually first, have the students list as many words or phrases as they can that are associated with each one. Write/list them on the board or on whatever presentation device you are using.
- Have the students look for "word pairs"---relationships between two words (one from each list). You can circle or highlight the words and draw a line to connect them. This will serve as a visual clue for the students and let you know which word associations have been identified. Try to do as many as you can.
- Ask the class, based on this activity, *"What do you think we're going to be reading about today?"*
- Introduce the article.

During

Hand out copies of the article and a highlighter to each student.

- Give the students time to preview and scan the entire article.
- Ask the students, *"What do you notice about this text?" "How is it organized?"*
- Go to the multiple choice questions and read the first question. Then ask the students to find the section of the article where the answer to that question can be found.
- Have the students read the section and highlight the sentence(s) that answers the question. They should then go back and write the correct answer to the multiple-choice question.
- They should proceed in this fashion, answering each question until all 10 are complete.

After

Go over the questions orally as a class. Then debrief the class by discussing the questions below.

- What did we do today?
- How did this help us with understanding and comprehension?
- What reading skills and strategies did you use?
- What did you learn? About yourself? About test taking? Etc.

: Resources

http://discoverer.prod.sirs.com/discoweb/disco/do/article?urn=urn%3Asirs%3AUS%3BARTICL E%3BART%3B0000176060

: Possible Extension Activities

1. This is a good lesson to do before any standardized assessment is administered to practice test-taking skills.

2. Have the students pick an article of choice to read and create original multiple-choice assessments to go along with it. The students can exchange articles and their student-generated test with one another. You can have the articles centered around an upcoming theme or unit as well. That would be a nice way to incorporate supplemental readings and meet individual student needs. You can use QAR questioning as a guide for students and you can also print off some examples from "Costa's Level of Questioning" from the Internet for the students to use.

3. Students can practice the same strategy when answering questions in the required class text.

CHAPTER FOUR

SECONDARY SAMPLE UNITS: ENGLISH & SOCIAL STUDIES

This chapter walks you through two units that were used at the secondary level. As you review these lessons, notice how the note-making strategies are dictated by the text and desired learning outcomes. The focus at the secondary level is just like that at the elementary level: thinking independently, comprehending and summarizing, and making personal connections all in order to synthesize the information. Students at the secondary level still need and benefit from guided practice with this very important and fundamental skill.

Secondary Social Studies: Economics Unit
Is This Crisis Good for America?

(This week long unit was designed for a high school study skills class that meets daily for 43 minutes)

: Goals/Objectives

- Students will investigate our current economic conditions, the events that lead to this and the implications for the future.

:: Skills and Standards

Reading Skills

Main Idea
Inferencing
Drawing Conclusions
Relevant Details

Writing Skills

Paragraph Structure
Descriptive writing
Word Choice
Sentence Structure

Pennsylvania Reading Standards

R 11. A. 2.1 Identify and apply the meaning of vocabulary in nonfiction
R 11. A. 2.3 Make inferences, draw conclusions, and make generalizations based on text
R 11. A. 2.4 Identify and explain main ideas and relevant details
R 11. A. 2.5 summarize a nonfictional text as a whole

Pennsylvania Economics Standards

6.1 Economic Systems
6.2 Market and Functions of Government
6.3 Scarcities and Choice

: Materials

Copy of the Time magazine & charging bull article for each student
Highlighters
Note-making sheets (inserted below)
Pens/pencils
Computer access

Lesson: Day One

Before

- Write the word "economy" on the board. Brainstorm (individually, pairs, small groups or as a class) words, phrases or images that come to mind.
- Share as a class
- Hand out *Charging Bull* article. Have students read the passage independently first.

During

- Hand out discussion questions sheet. Students can work independently or in small groups to complete (see sheet below).
- Share with the class.

After

- Have students respond to the following in writing, *"Describe the US economy's past, present and future"*.
- If time permits, have students share. Otherwise, you can start off the next class session sharing the responses.

: Resources

http://nyclovesnyc.blogspot.com/2009/03/charging-bull-aka-wall-street-bull.html (charging bull article)

http://www.time.com/time/printout/0,8816,1887728,00.html (Time economics article)

Discussion Questions

Name _____

1. Why do you think a bull was chosen to present our country's financial district?

2. What other animals do you think made the "top 3" list? Why?

3. If a new animal were to be put out there today, what animal should be chosen? Why?

4. What object do you think symbolizes our economy today? Why?

Lesson: Day Two

Before

- Have the students define the following terms using the dictionary as a guide: *ubiquitous, zeitgeist, copacetic.* They need to find the definition that fits the context the word is used in the article. Distribute the article and show the students where the words are located (pages 1, to the top of 3 is what we're working with today).
- Go over meanings as a class.

During

- Read and discuss section one of the article (the first 9 paragraphs). Students should fill out the note-making sheet below as they read. This can be done independently, with a partner, in small groups or as a class.

After

- Discuss what stood out for them and where they think the author will go with this article.
- Answer any questions they may have.
- Closure: final comments and reflection

Question Chart

Name _____

Question	Your Response
1. What is the *tone* of this article?	
2. What examples did the author use to help explain his message? Were they effective? Why or Why not?	
3. From what point of view is this article written? How do you know (what examples from the text support this)?	
4. What is the author's purpose in this introduction?	

Lesson: Day Three (This may take two days)

Before

- **Do Now**: Show and/or display an image of the Yin & Yang on the board. Ask the students to respond to the following in writing, *"What does this mean/symbolize?"* Explain that the author uses this symbol as a metaphor for the next section of the article that they are going to read today.
- Share responses/thoughts with the class.

During

- Read and discuss the article (with a partner, in small groups or individually) stopping after each paragraph or two to analyze what was being compared and understand the author's intended message. Students can highlight important words and phrases. I'd also have them summarize the paragraphs in a sentence or two and write it in the margin right on the article itself.

After

- After finishing section 2 of the article (the 6 paragraphs) have students create a cartoon strip to summarize the main idea of this section. They should include a written and a visual component for each square. This can be done with Comic Life if you have that application on your computer. Otherwise, students can use the template below to guide them through the process.
- Share cartoon strips with the class
- Display in the classroom or put them together to create a magazine/newspaper.

Economic Cartoon Strip

Name _____

(Title) _____

Lesson: Day Four

Before

- **Do Now:** Write the words "addiction & change" on the board. Have students
- respond to this in writing: *"What do these words mean to you? How do they relate to our current economic situation?"*
- Discuss and share as a class.

During

- Read and discuss the next section of the article, titled *Work the Program* (independently, with a partner, in a small group or as a class). Have students fill out the question response sheet as they read (see below).

After

- Discuss responses to questions. This can be done in small groups first and then share out with the entire class.

Question Response Sheet

Name _____

1. Do you think the American people are addicted to greed and financial excess?

2. The author compares our current economic state to recovering from an addiction. How are they similar? What comparisons would you make? Why?

3. What "changes" do you think will emerge? What "changes" need to happen to make things better?

Lesson: Day Five (This may take two days)

Before
- Have students bring in a current events article about the economy. If possible, take students to the library to locate articles from various resources.

During
- Students will find/locate an article of interest to them.
- Read & summarize the article using the 4 Square note-making sheet (see below—this
- incorporates all the strategies implemented throughout this unit).
- Tell the students to be prepared to share this information with the class. They can use any creative means available for the presentation.

After (Day Two)
- Students will present their articles in small groups or to the entire class (whatever you feel will work best).

4 Square Note-Making Sheet

Name _____

Key Words/Phrases	Connections (What does this remind me of?)
Summary	**Symbol/Illustration**

: Extensions

- Finish reading the rest of the article practicing comprehension strategies.
- Create a class magazine about our economy from a teenager's perspective. The students can write and research about topics of choice or ones determined by the teacher.
- Research various international economic systems and compare/contrast them to ours.
- Write letters to President Obama with suggestions on how we (teens in the US) can help/play an active role in our economic development.

Secondary English: Tenth Grade

: Goals/Objectives

Students will analyze how Laura Esquirel uses food as a metaphor in the novel, *Like Water For Chocolate.*

: Skills, Strategies, and Standards

Reading Skills

Analysis
Inference
Summarizing
Synthesis
Visualization
Character Analysis
Connections

Writing Skills

Paragraph Structure
Descriptive Language
Word Choice
Sentence Structure

Pennsylvania Standards

1.1 A - H
Learning to Read Independently
1.3 A - F
Reading, Analyzing, and Interpreting Literature
1.5 A - G
Quality of Writing
1.7 A - C
Characteristics of Function of the English Language

: Materials

Novel - *Like Water For Chocolate* by: Laura Esquirel
4" x 6" Index Cards
Access to a computer for food links (if available)
Copies of advertisements that involve food from magazines, newspapers, restaurants, etc. (if computer access is not available)

:: Lesson Plan

Before (*This will take one day/45 minute period***)**

* Have students respond to the following prompt in writing, *"List all the things, people, places, emotions, etc. you think of when you see or hear the word Spam—as in the food. Do the same thing for the word Caviar?"*
* Share responses as a class.
* Review what a metaphor is and have students give examples.
* Introduce the concept of food as a metaphor and explain how the author chose this literary technique to creatively convey her message.
* Practice identifying food as a metaphor. If you have access to a computer use the following links. If you do not have access to a computer, find some examples of commercials or advertisements from newspapers or magazines to share with the class. You can also have each student bring in one of his/her favorite advertisement/commercial and modify some of the questions below as a springboard for discussion.

   Milk Commercial Link: **http://www.youtube.com/watch?v=1zJg-V704AY**

   Sample questions to ask after viewing the link:

What happened in the commercial?
What did the milk represent? Why? How did you know?
What was the intended message in the commercial?
If you had to write a slogan to go along with this commercial, what would you say? Why?

   Junk Food Link: **http://www.youtube.com/watch? V=5Jlv1c-3JeM**

   Sample questions to ask after viewing the link:

What could the apple and cinnamon represent in life? (Friendship, it takes two to make a relationship work.)
What does the excess cheese represent? (Greed)
What is the intended message in the Cookie Crisp commercial? How did the food impact the wolf's behavior? What could this be a metaphor for? (Perseverance)

   Olive Garden Link: **http://www.youtube.com/watch?v=y4g5unKUjZw**

   Sample questions to ask after viewing the link a few times (it's fast):

There are three people in this commercial. Which meal do you think represents each one? Why? Explain your choice.

   Example Response:

Stuffed Rigatoni = Mom because it is found in all three meals and the mom is the backbone of every family.
Rigatoni & Sausage = is the dad because most men love "meat" items.
Rigatoni & Chicken = is the boy because he is a male teen.

   * At the end of this session, have the students respond in writing to the following question, *"What food are you most like and why? Or what food best represents you and your personality?"*

Why (however you want to phrase it). The idea is for them to connect on a personal level with this, which in turn will help them understand the use of food as a metaphor in the book.

During (*This will take one day/45 minute period to introduce*)
- "January"---have the students read the recipe and title in the beginning of the chapter and make predictions about it.
- Based on the title of the recipe and the ingredients listed, what do you think we'll read about in this section? Why do you think that?
- Share responses.
- Have students read "January" (this can be done independently, with a partner, as a class, or you can read it aloud to them, however you choose).
- Discuss as a class.
- Introduce "Recipe Reflections" summarizing activity (see below) and go over expectations as described. Remind them what a recipe card looks like; you might want to bring in some samples to show them. You can also make a sample on a 4"x6" index card using the January one provided on the "Recipe Reflection" sheet. All you would need to do is add a summary and a border or symbol.
- We've outlined a plan that one 10th grade teacher implemented that worked well for her and her students (see attached reflection sample).

After (*This can be done the day the reflections are due. This may take one 45-minute session*)
- Students will get into small groups and share their "Recipe Reflections". This can be done round robin style, or each student can read his/her recipe reflection. The group can identify which month it represents.
- Each group will pick the best ones from the group to share with the rest of the class.
- Students can respond in writing to a prompt provided by the teacher. Some examples include: *What did you learn about Tita during this time? What message is the author trying to convey in this section? Do you think she was successful? Why or why not?*
- When students respond to a prompt of this nature, have them cite at least 3 examples from the text to support their thinking.

: Resources

Food Links as listed above.

: Possible Extension Activities

* **"Restaurant Reflections"** ----the students can summarize/retell the story via their own original restaurant menus. They will have to give their restaurant a name (and they can't use *Like Water For Chocolate*), create a theme based menu listing the names of the food, beverages, desserts, appetizers and next to it in parenthesis make a reference to the book of who or what it represents (name of a character, setting, situation, etc). You can provide them with some actual samples to give them an idea of what the final project might look like. They can share their menus and restaurants in small groups and each group member can fill out a "restaurant review" as a form of assessment. You can create a rubric based on your desired expectations and outcomes.

* **Class Cookbook**---The class can compile a cookbook that represents each month of the novel. This is a nice culminating activity where each student's work can be showcased.

* **Cooking Show**---student can work in groups to create a segment of a cooking show. The students will be assigned a month and they would have to create an original recipe (that they would share in a cooking show format) that depicts their interpretation of what happened in the novel.

: References

N/A

Like Water for Chocolate

Recipe Reflections

On a weekly basis you will be asked to summarize and analyze each chapter assigned.
You will be given a 4x6 index card at the start of each week. The following are the components that
must be included in each "Recipe Reflection":

Lined side:
• One paragraph summary of chapter

On blank side:
* Recipe name and ingredients (include amounts) that metaphorically represent the characters, conflicts **and** events in each chapter.
* a graphic representation of the chapter elements and/or recipe (It should not need an explanation). It should be obvious and relate.)

Example for "January":

Sausage Sundae (Family Traditions left Tita feeling cold)

1 tbsp. Salt (Tita's tears)
1 lb. Sausage (Ranch life and family traditions)
1 gallon Vanilla Ice Cream (Rosaura b/c she's plain, common, and doesn't stand out.)
2 cups Chocolate Sauce (Pedro b/c he's the sweet man that wants to enhance and be a part of Tita's life)
1 Cherry (Nacha b/c she's the most important person to Tita & her presence always makes things right.)

Rubric:
  • Summary: 5 points
  • Recipe title & explanation: 3 points
  • Graphic representation: 2 points
  • Recipe ingredients and explanation: 10 points
  • TOTAL: 20 points

CHAPTER FIVE

SECONDARY RESOURCES

The goal of this chapter is to show you how to incorporate a variety of literacy strategies at the secondary level. The following strategies described can be easily incorporated into your curriculum:

- Key Words
- Charts
- Vocabulary Marketing
- 4 Square reflection for math
- I-Chart

Secondary Social Studies: Global Studies
Inside a Madrasa

:: Goals/Objectives

- Students will compare and contrast American and Pakistan schools.

:: Skills and Standards

Reading Skills

Main Idea
Inferencing
Drawing Conclusions
Relevant Details

Writing Skills

Paragraph Structure
Focus
Word Choice
Sentence Structure
Organization

Pennsylvania Standards

R 11. A. 2.3 Make inferences, draw conclusions, and make generalizations based on text
R 11. A. 2.4 Identify and explain main ideas and relevant details
R 11. A. 2.5 Summarize a nonfictional text as a whole

: Materials

Copy of the article for each student to use (see link below).
Teacher copy of the article
Note-making sheet
Pen/Pencil
Highlighters (if they want to highlight as they read)

Link:

http://discoverer.prod.sirs.com/discoweb/disco/do/article?urn=urn%3Asirs%3AUS%3BARTICLE%3BART%3B0000256935

:: Lesson Plan

Before

- *Do Now*: (Write this on the board or show it via your computer) Describe your typical school day. What do you like about it? What would you change if you could?
- Share responses as a class.
- Introduce the topic and article to the class.

During

- Have students read the article independently. As they read, have them fill out the note-making sheet to summarize and highlight the main idea of each section.
- Discuss the article and share note-making sheets.

After

Discuss and review the article.

- Highlight similarities and differences between the schools. This can be done via a Venn diagram or T-chart.
- Letter writing activity---have students write a letter to a student in a Madrasa. Possible brainstorming ideas are, *What would you share with him/her? What do you want to know or learn about their life, school, etc.? Remember you are representing the United States. What would you share about you and your life?*
- Or you may want to brainstorm topics/ideas as a class that can be included in their letters.
- Revisit the friendly letter format. You may want to provide an outline to help them organize their thoughts and make the letters flow.

: Resources

http://englishplus.com/grammar/00000144.htm

: Possible Extension Activities:

1. Exchange letters with an actual class in Pakistan if possible. If not, you can always swap letters within your own class. Have students research to find the answers to the questions asked in each letter. Each student will respond from the Pakistan perspective, and do his/her best to provide the reader with all the information requested.
2. Research and learn about schools around the world. Have students put together a Power Point presentation, or any project that involves a visual of some kind, and include a written component. Be sure that they include the purpose, function, and structure of the school, as well as how it meets the needs of the culture and community.
3. Students can research various schools and education in the United States. They can also learn more about Obama's educational reform goals, and what he wants for all American students. You may want to follow-up and have students write letters to President Obama with their views, opinions and suggestions. They can submit them to him via his website www.BarackObama.com.

Madrasa Note-Making Sheet

Name _____ Date _____

Sacred Text	A Long Tradition
Cultural Differences	**Religion Above All**
Key Words to Remember	**What stood out for me. ......**

Secondary Social Studies: Africa
Saharan Trade Route

:: Goals/Objectives

- Students will learn about the Saharan Trade Route and how it affected Africa's development.

:: Skills and Standards

Reading Skills

Main Idea
Inferencing
Drawing Conclusions
Relevant Details

Writing Skills

Paragraph Structure
Descriptive writing
Word Choice
Sentence Structure

Pennsylvania Standards

R 11. A. 2.1 Identify and apply the meaning of vocabulary in nonfiction
R 11. A. 2.3 Make inferences, draw conclusions, and make generalizations based on text
R 11. A. 2.4 Identify and explain main ideas and relevant details
R 11. A. 2.5 Summarize a nonfictional text as a whole

: Materials

Copy of the article for each student to use (see link below).
Teacher copy of the article
Highlighters
Key Words Activity sheet

Link:

http://web.ebscohost.com/src/delivery?vid=6&hid=6&sid=156be913-68db-42c2-9ce5-dc43d57cc958%40sessionmgr2

:: Lesson Plan

Before

Have students respond to the following in writing.

- **Do Now**: What types of trading was done in Africa? Provide examples and describe the impacts as well. Share responses.
- Show the map of trading routes in the Sahara Desert.
- Map link: http://www.mrdowling.com/images/609trade.gif
- Discuss the map and introduce the article (see link below).

During

Hand out copies of the article and a highlighter to each student.

- Give the students time to preview and scan the entire article.
- Ask the students, *"What do you notice about this text?"*, *"How is it organized?"*
- Hand out the "Key Words Activity Sheet".
- Students can work independently, with a partner or in small groups.
- After reading the article, debrief as a class. Ask what stood out for them. You may want to have them share their key words within small groups, and then have that group come up with a list of 5-10 "Key Words" for the article. You can also take this one step further and generate a class list of 5-10 "Key Words" for the article. This will generate a lot of discussion and aid with comprehension of the text.
- If you want, you can tell the students that they have to use the 5-10 "Key Words" generated by the class in the "After Reading Activity" they are doing.

After

Students will share their "After Reading Activity" with the class.

- You can generate a rubric to help assess their work.
- You may also want to modify the assignment to meet your individual class and student needs.

: Resources

- *Two Word Strategy*: Linda Hoyt's book Read, Revisit & Retell (1999) pgs 4-5.
- Africa Map Link: (http://www.mrdowling.com/images/609trade.gif)
- Article Link: (http://web.ebscohost.com/src/delivery?vid=6&hid=6&sid=156be913-68db-42c2-9ce5-dc43d57cc958%40sessionmgr2)
- Key Words Activity Sheet

: Possible Extension Activities

1. You can assign students different roles for the "After Reading Activity" exercise. This will require them to view this experience via a different point of view. You can assign one group to present like they were the traders, another group could represent the travelers, another one could be a ruler from one of the kingdoms, etc.

2. You can also assign the students the mode of advertising. One group can be CNN reporters and have to write and present in that genre/style. Another group could be from Time Magazine writing a current news piece on the Saharan Trade Route of Africa and the lasting impacts still felt today.

3. You may want to have students present using only visuals. This would be very challenging and very interesting. IT would be interesting to see the symbols/objects they choose to represent and summarize this text. Some examples: a mural, a rebus book, and photo album/scrapbook, music video, etc.

4. Students can create a class alphabet book about African Trading---this sounds simple, but is extremely effective. This really forces the students to refine their thinking and word choice. This is "summarization" at its finest.

Key Words Activity

Name _____

Read the article. As you read, write down one or two words that best summarize each section. The word can be from the text or can be any word that you feel is appropriate. Write them in the boxes below.

Word Bank

After Reading: If you had to advertise this article as a television documentary, movie, or book how would you do it? What would you say? What words from the word bank would be necessary to include? Be creative, have fun and remember you are trying to get people to want to watch or read about it.

Secondary Global Studies: China

:: Goal/Objective:

This is an example of how to structure writing from a note-making strategy to a five-paragraph essay. This was done with a group of tenth graders while they were learning about the heritage of China.

Note-Making Sheet: This was used as they worked through a chapter in their textbooks.

Concept	Main Idea	Symbol	One word summary
Confucius			
Daoism			
Legalism			
Buddhism			

Section Two Open-Ended Prompt

Name _____

In section two, we learned about Confucianism, Daoism, Legalism and Buddhism. If you had to choose one as a guiding principle of how you would live your life, which one would you choose and why?

Open-Ended Prompt Writing Outline

Name _____

Introduction (1ˢᵗ Paragraph):

Body (2ⁿᵈ, 3ʳᵈ & 4ᵗʰ Paragraphs):

Reason	Specific Example
1.	
2.	
3.	

Conclusion (5ᵗʰ Paragraph):

Introduction to Research: I-Chart

Goal/Objective:

This is an adaptation of James Hoffman's work. It is a note-making strategy that students can use as an introduction or beginning step in conducting research. Teachers have given this to students before they go to the library or get on the computers to gather information. This helps to guide them through the process, and provides a layer of accountability as well.

The idea of an I-Chart is for students to start with a question that they would like to learn more about and write it on the "topic" line. As the students conduct their preliminary research, they fill out the rest of the chart to begin to help organize their work and thoughts. This can be used with students working individually or those working with partners/small groups. It can be modified and adapted to fit your own particular needs or areas of interest.

I-Chart

Name/s: _____

Topic: _____

What I/we already know about this topic:

What I learned:

1.

2.

3.

4.

5.

6.

Other interesting facts:

1.

2.

3.

Key Words:

1.

2.

3.

4.

Resources: (Where did you find your information?)

New Question to research based on what was learned today:

Did you get a VISUAL??????????????

Secondary Math: 4 Square Reflection Sheet

:: <u>Goal/Objective</u>: This can be used to help students reflect individually or as a group after problem solving exercises.

Key Words/Phrases (Found in the problem or needed to solve the problem)	Show your work (In this space show how you solved the problem)
Connections (Have you seen this before? How can you use this in life?)	Summary (Explain what you did and how you arrived at your answer/solution. Highlight the skills and strategies used.)

Breinigsville, PA USA
17 November 2009
227772BV00002B/2/P